FROM:

CARPE DiEM

Compiled by Evelyn Beilenson
Introduction by Amber Tunnell
Illustrated by Sarajo Frieden

PETER PAUPER PRESS, INC.
White Plains, New York

Illustrations © 2013 Sarajo Frieden/Lilla Rogers

Designed by Margaret Rubiano

Copyright © 2013
Peter Pauper Press, Inc.
202 Mamaroneck Avenue
White Plains, NY 10601
All rights reserved
ISBN 978-1-4413-1329-4
Printed in China
7 6 5 4

Visit us at www.peterpauper.com

CARPE DIEM

We have only this moment,
sparkling like a star in our hand.

FRANCIS BACON

In this high-octane life of myriad distractions,
it's easy to forget that each moment is an
instant of our life we will never get back.
The Roman poet Horace had it right when
he penned the Latin phrase, *Carpe diem*,
or "Seize the day." This little testament
to the Here and Now, packed with jewels
of wisdom from a diversity of icons, from

Mary Shelley to Steve Jobs, will inspire you to fully engage every moment—to never rely on tomorrow when it comes to your life today. Right now is perfect. Go climb Mount Everest. Chase after the career you've always wanted. Visit Paris. Buy your loved one a present. Shine on! And remember: It's never too late to make your life extraordinary.

CARPE DIEM!

TODAY IS THE FIRST AND LAST DAY OF FOREVER.

STEPHENIE MEYER

If we would only give, just once, the same amount of reflection to what we want to get out of life that we give to the question of what to do with a two weeks' vacation, we would be startled at our false standards and the aimless procession of our busy days.

DOROTHY CANFIELD FISHER

Waste your
money and you're
only out of money,
but waste your time
and you've lost a
part of your life.

MICHAEL LEBOEUF

TODAY, FILL YOUR CUP OF LIFE WITH SUNSHINE AND LAUGHTER.

DODINSKY

Carpe diem.
Seize the
day, boys.
Make your
lives
extraordinary.

JOHN KEATING IN
DEAD POETS SOCIETY

GO FOR IT NOW.
THE FUTURE
IS PROMISED
TO NO ONE.

WAYNE DYER

The clock is running.
Make the most of today.
Time waits for no man.
Yesterday is history.
Tomorrow is a mystery.
Today is a gift. That's why
it is called the present.

ALICE MORSE EARLE

There is a time for
risky love. There is a time for
extravagant gestures.
There is a time to pour out
your affections on one you love.
And when the time comes—
seize it, don't miss it.

MAX LUCADO

EVERY SECOND IS OF INFINITE VALUE.

JOHANN WOLFGANG VON GOETHE

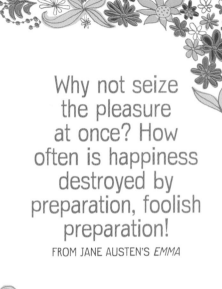

Why not seize
the pleasure
at once? How
often is happiness
destroyed by
preparation, foolish
preparation!

FROM JANE AUSTEN'S *EMMA*

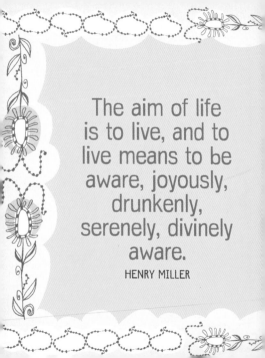

The aim of life
is to live, and to
live means to be
aware, joyously,
drunkenly,
serenely, divinely
aware.

HENRY MILLER

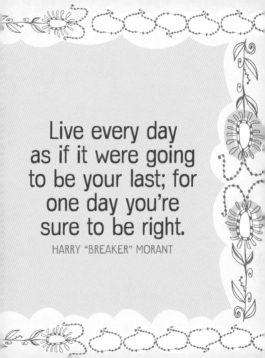

Live every day
as if it were going
to be your last; for
one day you're
sure to be right.

HARRY "BREAKER" MORANT

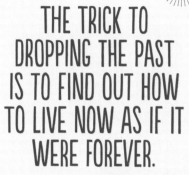

THE TRICK TO
DROPPING THE PAST
IS TO FIND OUT HOW
TO LIVE NOW AS IF IT
WERE FOREVER.

DEEPAK CHOPRA

REAL GENEROSITY TOWARD THE FUTURE LIES IN GIVING ALL TO THE PRESENT.

ALBERT CAMUS

Why always,
"not yet"? Do
flowers in spring
say, "not yet"?

NORMAN DOUGLAS

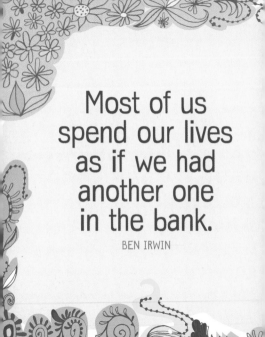

Most of us
spend our lives
as if we had
another one
in the bank.

BEN IRWIN

EVERY DAY IS
AN OPPORTUNITY
TO MAKE A NEW
HAPPY ENDING.

AUTHOR UNKNOWN

We seem to be going
through a period of nostalgia
now and everyone seems to think
yesterday was better than today. I
personally don't think it was, and
I would advise you not to wait ten
years from now before admitting
today was great. If you're hung
up on nostalgia, pretend today is
yesterday and just go out and
have one hell of a time.

ART BUCHWALD

THE BEGINNING
IS ALWAYS TODAY.

MARY SHELLEY

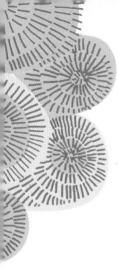

Life moves
pretty fast.
If you don't
stop and look
around once
in a while, you
could miss it.

FROM *FERRIS BUELLER'S
DAY OFF*

YESTERDAY IS ASHES; TOMORROW WOOD. ONLY TODAY DOES THE FIRE BURN BRIGHTLY.

ESKIMO PROVERB

You must live in the present,
launch yourself on every
wave, find your eternity in
each moment. Fools stand on
their island of opportunities
and look toward another land.
There is no other land, there
is no other life but this.

HENRY DAVID THOREAU

Security in a relationship
lies neither in looking back
to what was in nostalgia,
nor forward to what it might
be in dread or anticipation,
but living in the present
relationship and accepting
it as it is now.

ANNE MORROW LINDBERGH

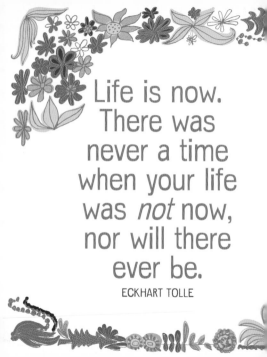

Life is now.
There was
never a time
when your life
was *not* now,
nor will there
ever be.

ECKHART TOLLE

DAY, *N:* A PERIOD OF TWENTY-FOUR HOURS, MOSTLY MISSPENT

AMBROSE BIERCE

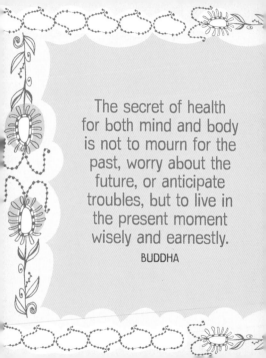

The secret of health for both mind and body is not to mourn for the past, worry about the future, or anticipate troubles, but to live in the present moment wisely and earnestly.

BUDDHA

With the past,
I have nothing
to do; nor
with the future.
I live now.

RALPH WALDO EMERSON

THE TIME FOR ACTION IS NOW. IT'S NEVER TOO LATE TO DO SOMETHING.

CARL SANDBURG

Today is life—the only
life you are sure of. Make the
most of today. Get interested in
something. Shake yourself awake.
Develop a hobby. Let the winds
of enthusiasm sweep through
you. Live today with gusto.

DALE CARNEGIE

Each day comes
bearing its
own gifts. Untie
the ribbons.

RUTH ANN SCHABACKER

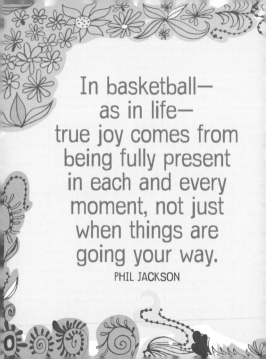

In basketball—
as in life—
true joy comes from
being fully present
in each and every
moment, not just
when things are
going your way.

PHIL JACKSON

TODAY IS
THE FIRST DAY
OF THE REST OF
YOUR LIFE.

CHARLES DEDERICH

I believe you
should live each
day as if it is your last,
which is why I don't
have any clean laundry,
because, come on,
who wants to wash
clothes on the last
day of their life?

AUTHOR UNKNOWN

ONE TODAY
IS WORTH TWO
TOMORROWS.

BENJAMIN FRANKLIN

FOREVER— IS COMPOSED OF NOWS.

EMILY DICKINSON

Do not say, "It is morning," and dismiss it with a name of yesterday. See it for the first time as a newborn child that has no name.

RABINDRANATH TAGORE

Bringing people into
the here-and-now. The real
universe. That's the present
moment. The past is no good
to us. The future is full of
anxiety. Only the present
is real—the here-and-now.
Seize the day.

FROM SAUL BELLOW'S *SEIZE THE DAY*

The other day a man
asked me what I
thought was the best
time of life. "Why,"
I answered without
a thought, "Now."

DAVID GRAYSON

Listen to the Exhortation
of the Dawn!
Look to this Day! For it is Life,
The very Life of Life. . . .
For Yesterday is but a Dream,
And Tomorrow is only a Vision;

But Today well lived
Makes every Yesterday
a Dream of Happiness,
And every Tomorrow a Vision of Hope.
Look well therefore to this Day!
Such is the Salutation of the Dawn!

KĀLIDĀSA

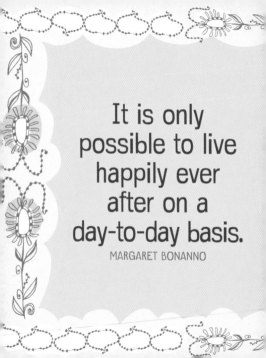

It is only
possible to live
happily ever
after on a
day-to-day basis.

MARGARET BONANNO

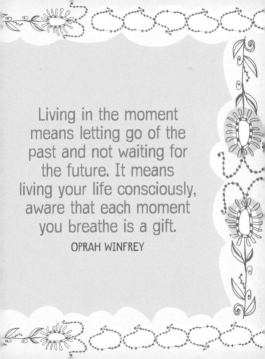

Living in the moment
means letting go of the
past and not waiting for
the future. It means
living your life consciously,
aware that each moment
you breathe is a gift.

OPRAH WINFREY

Realize deeply that the present moment is all you ever have. Make the Now the primary focus of your life.

ECKHART TOLLE

Time is free, but it's priceless. You can't own it, but you can use it. You can't keep it, but you can spend it. Once you've lost it you can never get it back.

HARVEY MACKAY

IT'S NOT "WHAT IF?" IT'S "WHAT NOW?"

AUTHOR UNKNOWN

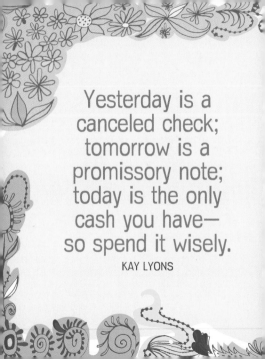

Yesterday is a canceled check; tomorrow is a promissory note; today is the only cash you have— so spend it wisely.

KAY LYONS

For every
minute you are
angry you lose
sixty seconds
of happiness.

RALPH WALDO EMERSON

For the past 33 years, I have looked in the mirror every morning and asked myself: "If today were the last day of my life, would I want to do what I am about to do today?" And whenever the answer has been "No" for too many days in a row, I know I need to change something.

STEVE JOBS

WORRY DOES NOT EMPTY TOMORROW OF ITS SORROW, IT EMPTIES TODAY OF ITS STRENGTH.

CORRIE TEN BOOM

BE HERE NOW.

RAM DASS

Life is always walking
up to us and saying,
"Come on in, the living's
fine," and what do
we do? Back off and
take its picture.

RUSSELL BAKER

Get action.
Seize the moment.
Man was never
intended to become
an oyster.

THEODORE ROOSEVELT

I wanted to convince
you that you must learn to
make every act count, since
you are going to be here
for only a short while, in fact,
too short for witnessing all
the marvels of it.

CARLOS CASTANEDA

Dream as if you'll live forever. Live as if you'll die today.

JAMES DEAN

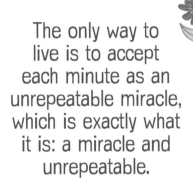

The only way to
live is to accept
each minute as an
unrepeatable miracle,
which is exactly what
it is: a miracle and
unrepeatable.

MARGARET STORM JAMESON

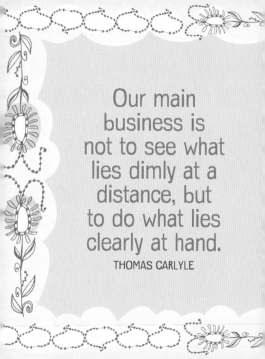

Our main business is not to see what lies dimly at a distance, but to do what lies clearly at hand.

THOMAS CARLYLE

To change one's life: Start immediately. Do it flamboyantly. No exceptions.

WILLIAM JAMES

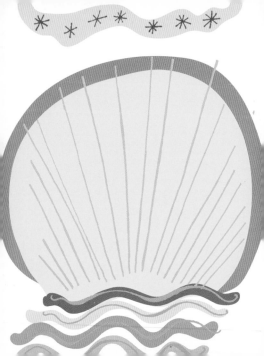

BELIEVE THAT
EACH DAY THAT
SHINES ON YOU
IS YOUR LAST.

HORACE

Open yourself up
to what is in front
of you rather than
allowing yourself
to be distracted.

DEEPAK CHOPRA

I try to learn from
the past, but I plan
for the future by
focusing exclusively
on the present. That's
where the fun is.

DONALD TRUMP

Begin doing
what you want to
do now. We are not living
in eternity. We have only
this moment, sparkling
like a star in our hand—
and melting like
a snowflake.

FRANCIS BACON

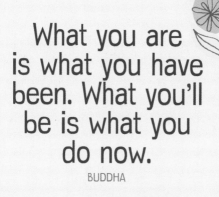

What you are
is what you have
been. What you'll
be is what you
do now.

BUDDHA

Now is the only time.
How we relate to it creates
the future. In other words, if
we're going to be more
cheerful in the future, it's because
of our aspiration and exertion
to be cheerful in the present.
What we do accumulates; the
future is the result of what
we do right now.

PEMA CHÖDRÖN

You'll seldom experience
regret for anything that
you've done. It is what
you haven't done that will
torment you. The message,
therefore, is clear. Do it!...
Seize every second of
your life and savor it. Value
your present moments.

WAYNE DYER

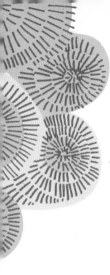

Beset by
a difficult
problem? Now
is your chance
to shine. Pick
yourself up,
get to work,
and get
triumphantly
through it.

RALPH MARSTON

ALL THE WINDOWS
OF MY HEART I
OPEN TO THE DAY.

JOHN GREENLEAF WHITTIER

YOU ONLY LIVE ONCE,
BUT IF YOU DO IT RIGHT,
ONCE IS ENOUGH.

MAE WEST

WHY NOT JUST LIVE IN THE MOMENT, ESPECIALLY IF IT HAS A GOOD BEAT?

GOLDIE HAWN

"What day is it?"
asked Pooh.
"It's today,"
squeaked Piglet.
"My favorite day,"
said Pooh.

A. A. MILNE

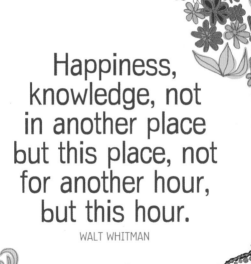

Happiness,
knowledge, not
in another place
but this place, not
for another hour,
but this hour.

WALT WHITMAN

Carpe Diem!
"Seize the Day!"
HORACE